DATE DUE

TRACK & FIELD
THE JUMPS

MORGAN HUGHES

The Rourke Press, Inc.
Vero Beach, Florida 32964

© 2001 The Rourke Press, Inc.

Morgan Hughes is a sports writer who has covered professional hockey, baseball, tennis and cycling. He has written several childrens books, both fiction and nonfiction, and is currently at work on his first full-length novel.

PROJECT ADVISOR:
Richard Roberts is the former head track and field coach at Florida State University, where he was also a star athlete during his undergraduate studies. He resides in Tallahassee with his wife and three hunting dogs.

PHOTO CREDITS:
All photos by Ryals Lee, Jr.

ILLUSTRATIONS:
Matt Willard, Kingfish Studio (page 4, 23)

EDITORIAL SERVICES: Janice L. Smith for Penworthy

Library of Congress Cataloging-in-Publication Data

Hughes, Morgan, 1957-
    Track and field / Morgan E. Hughes.
       p. cm.
    Include indexes.
    Contents: [1] An Introduction to Track & Field — [2] The sprints — [3] Middle and long distance runs — [4] The jumps — [5] The throws — [6] Training and fitness.
       ISBN 1-57103-288-6 (v. 1). — ISBN 1-57103-291-6 (v. 2). — ISBN 1-57103-289-4 (v. 3). — ISBN 1-57103-290-8 (v. 4). — ISBN 1-57103-292-4 (v. 5). — ISBN 1-57103-293-2 (v. 6)
    1. Track-athletics Juvenile literature. [1. Track and field.] I. Title.
GV1060.5.H833 1999
796.42—dc21   99-20284
                                                                    CIP

Printed in the USA

TABLE OF CONTENTS

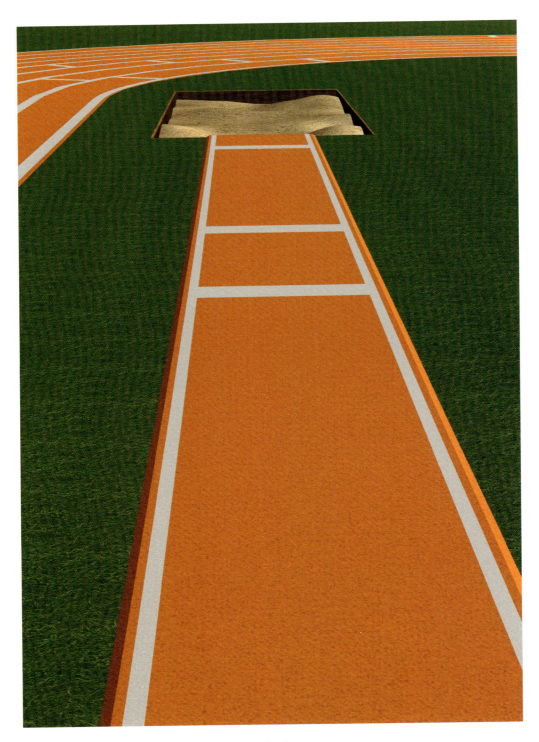

The long jump track leads to a sand pit.

THE LONG JUMP

One of the most exciting events in track and field is the running long jump. It combines blistering speed, the grace of flight, and the thrill of "sticking the landing." And, of course, all of these elements must be put together with split-second timing.

The running long jump specialist has one objective: to sprint down the approach **runway**, hit the small, rectangular **takeoff board** without fouling (stepping over the line), and launch his or her body into the air.

As they become airborne, long jumpers must catapult themselves as far as they can over the **scoring zone**—a sand pit about 10 feet (3 meters) wide and 20 feet (6 meters) long. Long jumpers must extend their legs and position their feet for a strong, controlled landing. The distance of a successful long jump is measured from the takeoff board's forward edge to the spot where the jumper's feet first touch the sand—unless another part of the jumper's body touches behind that spot.

Two rules hold true for the long jump. The faster you sprint down the runway, the better chance you'll have to leap high in the air. And the higher you leap in the air on takeoff, the farther you'll fly over the landing pit.

★ **DID YOU KNOW?**

In 1991, U.S. track and field star Mike Powell set a world record when he long jumped 29 feet, 4.5 inches (8.9 meters).

Long jumpers must be good sprinters.

If a long jumper steps over the white foul line, the jump is disqualified.

The rules of track and field don't limit the length of a long jumper's approach. The jumper should use as much of the runway as is needed to reach his or her best speed. The time and distance it takes for an athlete to achieve that speed may vary, so the length of the approach will vary.

An easy way to figure out how long your approach should be is to start at the takeoff board and sprint away from the sand pit. Have a coach or a friend mark the spot on the runway where you reach a full, controlled sprint. This should be your starting point.

The approach may be adjusted over time as you develop as a jumper. As you improve, it is likely that the length of your approach—the number of steps taken—will increase. At each phase of development, however, your approach should consist of exactly the same number of steps every time you do it.

As you sprint down the runway, you should try to relax and think "smooth." Your upper body and head should be as still and steady as possible. This will help you focus on the takeoff. Your first few steps may be rather slow, but you should quickly achieve proper speed. As you reach the takeoff board, raise your chin and thrust your chest forward. This will put you in a more "upward" posture as you get ready to launch. Before you take your first jump, practice the approach until you don't have to think about it anymore.

Just as important as the approach is the takeoff. This is the first place where a mistake—a foul—can cost you the jump. Rules specify that the long jumper must hit the takeoff board, an area which measures four feet (about 1.25 meters) wide by eight inches (about 20 centimeters) deep, with one foot (the plant foot) before leaping through the air.

On takeoff, the jumper's foot may touch in front of the board (in which case the jumper will lose distance), but if the foot goes beyond the far edge of the board, the jumper has fouled and the jump is not counted.

Forward momentum is more important than height.

Feet and hands outstretched, the long jumper prepares to land.

In most competitions, each jumper has three chances to record a best jump in an effort to make it to the final round of three more jumps. Foot fouls can ruin the day.

Hitting the takeoff board is the "moment of truth." A smooth, relaxed plant on the board will allow the jumper to keep all forward progress—momentum—headed in the right direction. A heavy plant on the board will have the opposite effect, stopping forward progress and limiting the distance of the jump.

There are two acceptable mid-air positions: the hang and the hitch kick. In the beginning, jumpers should master the hang style, where they maintain the position they are in as they leave the takeoff board until they extend legs and feet for landing. The hitch kick, in which the jumper appears to be running in midair after takeoff, is more complicated and can be learned when the young jumper moves to the high school level.

THE TRIPLE JUMP

Like the running long jump, the triple jump demands
three key elements: speed, strength, and coordination.
Once called the "hop, step, and jump," this event adds
another element to the running long jump: a pair of
intermediate strides—the hop and step—that come after
the jumper has launched from the takeoff board.

In the running long jump, there is one takeoff and one landing. In the triple jump there are three takeoffs and three landings. Each of these must be performed without losing any speed or momentum.

The triple jump is performed on the same runway and with the same sand pit landing area as the running long jump. The approach for the triple jump is similar to the approach for the running long jump and must be done with the same precision.

In the triple, the jumper must reach the takeoff board with his or her strongest leg forward. This leg will support the jumper for the first two intermediate strides. The first of the three phases, the hop, begins when you hit the takeoff board with your stronger leg. At takeoff, the arm that corresponds to the takeoff leg will be in a forward position. Instead of leaping high into the air as a long jumper does, you will stay closer to the ground to remain in control for the rest of the jump.

While airborne, bring your arms back behind your hips, elbows bent, as your takeoff leg comes forward. Your knee should be high and bent to prepare for a second jump off that same leg. As your foot hits to begin the second phase, or step, thrust your arms forward and up to launch a second attempt for greatest distance.

COACH'S CORNER

Speed and strength are by far the more visible qualities of a successful triple jumper. Just as important, however, is balance, without which no amount of speed or strength can deliver a winning jump.

The triple jumper launches off her right leg.

Exploding forward, the triple jumper prepares for the first landing.

While airborne, once again bring your arms back behind your hips, elbows bent. This time, the lead knee will remain high and bent as you prepare to start the third, or jump, phase. With the "hop" and "step" completed, you must now leap as high and far as you can, using the hang techniques described for running long jumpers.

As you near the sand, extend your legs and feet in front of you, with your heels as close together as possible. Once you hit the sand, your hands will swing back and your knees will bend to absorb the shock. At that moment, thrust your arms forward to maintain your momentum toward the end of the pit. If you fall backward, your jump will be measured from the point of your body which lands closest to the takeoff board, resulting in a shorter jump.

★ **DID YOU KNOW?**

At the 1996 Summer Olympic Games, Missouri's Kenny Harrison became the fifth American man—and the third in the last four Olympics—to win a gold medal in the triple jump.

It's important to practice the hop-step-jump sequence and to make each step about the same distance in length. The second phase of the triple jump is the hardest to learn and is usually the weakest portion of the jump. It must be practiced until it is as solid as the other phases.

The triple jumper tries to limit height while "hopping" as far as possible.

With the final approach to the landing pit, all energy is forced forward.

Some coaches suggest that beginners first practice the hop-step-jump sequence without the high-speed approach. This helps young track athletes develop the correct pace and rhythm of the complex action. After the three-step pattern is mastered, the sprint approach and the landing can be added.

To protect against possible injury, one very useful piece of equipment for both the running long jumper and the triple jumper is the heel guard. This plastic "cup" fits inside the track shoe and adds support to the heel, which absorbs a lot of shock. The heel cup won't help you jump farther, but it may prevent injury.

THE HIGH JUMP

In purely scientific terms, high jumping can be defined as "the conversion of **horizontal velocity** into **vertical lift**." But what does this mean to the budding track athlete?

In simpler terms, "horizontal velocity" is running speed, a key in almost every track and field event. This running speed comes during the high jumper's approach. At the end of the approach, the forward momentum of this horizontal velocity must then be transferred into the jump, or vertical lift. Of course, this is a tricky technique to learn and it requires several factors to be in place.

The goal of the high jumper is to leap over a horizontal bar set at various heights between two uprights no less than 12 feet (about 3.5 meters) apart. The bar's height is adjusted during competition after each jumper in the field has either "passed" at a given height or attempted to clear the bar. Jumpers are eliminated when they fail to clear a given height in the three allotted attempts. Knocking the bar off its pegs or breaking the imaginary plane between the bar and the ground are both causes for a jump to be disqualified.

Unlike the long jump, the triple jump, and the pole vault (see Chapter Four), the high jump does not feature a long sprint approach to the takeoff area.

Instead the high jumper approaches the bar at a controlled speed (arrived at by trial and error) within a square or rectangular apron. The angled approach that once served the traditional "scissor" and "straddle" jumps has been replaced by a curving arc, or **"J-hook,"** approach.

★ DID YOU KNOW?

Since its creation in the 1960s, the Fosbury Flop has become the most popular jump style in the high jump. It may feel odd to turn your back as you take off, but this is the most efficient technique for clearing the bar.

The high jump field consists of an approach area which leads to a
horizontal bar supported by two uprights.

The high jumper approaches the bar in a curving arc.

The landing pit is large (about 16 x 13 feet or 5 x 4 meters) and should be thickly padded with foam rubber to protect jumpers from injury. Of the several jumping styles, the **Fosbury Flop** is the most popular. However, all jumping styles have awkward landing positions.

In high jumping, strength and body type are equally important. Strength, particularly in the legs, is vital to achieving vertical lift—the leap. And history has shown that those athletes with certain body types—especially taller athletes—may make better high jumpers.

A taller athlete, given equal strength and technique, will have more success. The key to success is raising your center of gravity. A taller athlete already has a higher center of gravity and thus a built-in advantage.

In some ways, the run-up in high jumping is the same as the approach in the other jumping events. It must be tailored to each athlete's speed and timing, and it must be executed with the same precision every time.

If you use the Fosbury Flop, your run-up will start to the side rather than go directly at the bar. You'll approach toward the nearest upright. As you get close, you'll veer in a hooking pattern toward the center of the bar.

As always, proper technique is the most important element of this difficult event. As you know from many other sports—basketball, football, or volleyball—the ability to jump higher than your competitors can give you a definite edge.

In high jumping, a beginner must set a goal of being able to jump at least one foot (30 centimeters) higher than his or her own height. So, if you're five feet (1.52 meters) tall, you must strive to be able to clear a bar set at six feet (1.82 meters), and so on. In the end, it doesn't matter how tall you are or how fast you can run if you don't master the skills of takeoff and clearing the bar.

With high knee lift, the jumper swings his arms forward to gain height.

Once the hips have cleared the bar, the legs snap forward.

On takeoff, if you're a left-footed jumper, you'll plant your left foot as your body continues in the "J" and becomes sideways to the bar. The takeoff continues as the right knee drives upward and rotates to the left, turning your body. Both arms, with elbows bent, assist the movement by driving upward. This completes the necessary rotation for the jumper's backside to face the bar at the highest point. Once in the air, you will assume the back "lay-out" position (lying flat in midair) and thrust your hips upward. Bring your arms next to the hips, making sure not to lower them into the bar.

As your midsection clears the bar, bring your head up and bend forward at the waist while straightening your legs. This will force your legs up and over the bar.

It's important to relax through this jump, especially on the landing, which should be absorbed by your shoulders and upper back. This technique should never be attempted without proper landing equipment and expert supervision.

THE POLE VAULT

Just 40 years ago pole vaults in excess of 15 feet (4.5 meters) high were reason for worldwide celebration. In the mid-1990s, Russian pole vaulter Sergei Bubka set a series of world records by regularly vaulting more than 20 feet (6 meters) in height.

Women have begun competing in the pole vault only in the last decade or so, and have now established a world record of more than 15 feet (4.5 meters).

Some of the changes in pole vaulting have come as a result of improved training techniques. Most of the change, however, is due to technological advancements in equipment. Hickory, ash, bamboo, and steel poles have been replaced by poles made of high-tech fiberglass materials which make poles lighter, stronger, and more flexible.

Most experts believe pole vaulting is the hardest field event to analyze. It has some dangerous elements and should never be practiced without a coach.

Speed is a vital part of a winning vault. The faster you go when you plant for takeoff, the more bend or flex you'll get from the pole and the more height you'll gain.

Strength is also vital. A vaulter must be able to carry the pole, stick the plant, and hold on tight during takeoff.

Another factor that makes pole vaulting unique is that the recent developments in fiberglass poles have added an element of gymnastics to the foundation of strength and speed needed for successful vaulting. Good body control may help a vaulter clear heights even when mistakes have been made in the carry, the approach, or the plant. In the carry, the pole should be carried with the right hand palm up and the left hand palm down. The tip of the pole should be above eye level as you begin the run. Your back arm should be straight. Your hands should be 18 to 36 inches (45 to 90 centimeters) apart, depending on your size.

★ **DID YOU KNOW?**

Studies show that the best vaulters are those who started early so if you think you'll enjoy this thrilling event, it's a good idea to get started right away.

As the vaulter approaches, the pole is slanted slightly across his body.

The plant requires great arm strength.

Most vaulters use an approach distance of between 120 and 150 feet (35 and 45 meters). The key, as with all approaches, is consistency and control in the proper upright body position. The pole is awkward to carry, so it may take you a few strides to gain top speed. With each stride, your thighs should be parallel to the ground. Remember, you want to run *through* not just *to,* the **plant box**.

As you reach the plant box, lower the tip of the pole and curl your back hand until it's just in front of your face and the pole is at eye level.

As you plant the tip of the pole in the plant box, your shoulders are square to the bar and your right hand is over your takeoff foot. Your right arm is high. The swing and **rock back** are next. As you bring your hips forward and up, you transfer your horizontal—running—speed into vertical lift, or height. The rock back sees the right knee drive forward while the straight left leg swings forward to catch up until the hips are between your head and the bar.

★ DID YOU KNOW?

For athletes in the 10-12 age group, pole vaulting should remain an "introductory" activity (that is, one of many you try). Once you're 13 or older, you can begin to specialize.

The rock back accomplishes the necessary stress needed to bend the pole. When the pole has reached its maximum bend, it will recoil. In proper position, you will ride the recoil and gain vertical lift. When your feet are at their highest point, you begin the pull, turn, and release.

On the "lift," the vaulter swings his feet toward the bar.

Once over the bar, the vaulter is careful to push his pole away.

First you use your arms to pull yourself even higher as the pole straightens. Then you rotate (turn) your body so that the bar passes in front of your stomach and not your back. Feet first, you will arc over the top of the bar, then release the pole one hand at a time—lower hand first, then your top hand.

It is important to make sure the pole doesn't knock the bar from its pegs. Otherwise your vault will not count.

Once over the top, you must relax your body for the fall to the landing pad. Although the pad is designed to ensure your safety, it's still important to hit the pad loose and relaxed.

With all the advancements in poles and the common sight of vaulters bending their poles nearly in half, it's important to remember to use as stiff a pole as you can. The stiffer the pole, the higher the vault. You may change poles as you improve since the pole you feel comfortable with will depend on your technique, strength, and speed.

As with the high jump, proper landing equipment is absolutely necessary every time you vault, as is expert supervision.

TRAINING TIPS

Overall fitness and conditioning are important for all track and field participants. Due to the technical nature of the jumps, however, specific drills or exercises are necessary to perfect the skills called into play.

For the Long Jump

In training sessions, work on each segment of the running long jump. The approach must be mastered before the other elements. The height and distance of your jumps will improve with practice.

The jumper needs speed, strength, and technique. Some common exercises include (1) jogging and easy warm-up runs, (2) stretching and bending, (3) weight training—half squats and leg presses, (4) sets of 50- and 60-meter sprints, (5) longer runs of up to 300 **meters**, and (6) low hurdling.

Certain drills will help the long jumper practice the elements of his or her event. "Pop-ups," for example, feature a short approach to takeoff—as few as five to eight strides—and focus on the proper takeoff form and lift.

You will also practice full approaches so you can master all the check marks on the runway—the spots you use to determine if your run up to the takeoff board is "on schedule."

Of course, you will also combine these elements for repeated full-scale long jumps. But remember, the more you prepare each segment, the better the jump will be in total.

For the Triple Jump

The triple jumper and the long jumper often train side by side. In many instances the exercises they use to build strength and endurance are the same. In particular, exercises that develop the knees, ankles, abdomen, and back are vital for jumpers in both events.

★ COACH'S CORNER

When training for the triple jump, be aware of such errors as:
(1) an inconsistent stride,
(2) hopping too high,
(3) over-rotating on launch,
(4) twisting in midair, and
(5) poor hand-leg coordination.

The triple jumper needs strong knees, ankles, and abdominals.

The high jumper practices his plant and launch without a bar.

However, the triple jumper also must focus on some special exercises for this event. They include (1) sets of hops and steps from a standing position, with emphasis on lifting the knees high on each hop and flexing the leg on landing; (2) hopping for up to ten repetitions (reps) on each leg; (3) hops and long steps working up to ten repetitions and improving distance within those reps, while alternating legs and building speed; (4) hopping and stepping to the sand pit using a short approach—as few as eight to ten strides; and (5) sets of the hop-step-jump sequence to stress rhythm and smoothness.

For the High Jump

You need to be in good shape for this demanding event. You want to be light on your feet and also have explosive power in your legs. Some training exercises include (1) light jogging; (2) stretching and bending, primarily the back and hips; (3) skipping rope for agility; (4) strength training for the legs; (5) sprinting, bounding, and hurdling for power.

As you become comfortable with the techniques needed for proper approach and takeoff, as well as those needed to clear the bar, your imperfections will be more easily corrected.

⭐ **DID YOU KNOW?**

Your head weighs up to 10 pounds (4.5 grams). Use the weight to help you over the bar by holding up your chin. If you drop or turn your chin, you can change the direction of your body on the jump.

You will do short-approach jumps of about three or four steps to improve technique and develop power in your takeoff.

With your coach, you'll determine if your takeoff mark is too close to or too far from the bar and if your angle of approach is right—particularly with the J-hook style. You will also decide if your approach is smooth enough, your stride even, and your body relaxed.

High jumpers should work on staying relaxed throughout the jump.

Many repetitions and "walk throughs" help the vaulter master the plant.

You will work on the takeoff—especially the foot plant—and find where corrections can be made to help you jump higher and more gracefully.

For the Pole Vault

For any successful pole vaulter, strength in the arms, legs, stomach, and shoulders is crucial. You will want to include sit-ups and pull-ups in any exercise program you begin, along with strength training in those areas.

Practicing the approach—with the pole—is very important as well, as you want to perfect the timing and precision of your strides and your pole plant. Running without the pole—doing sprints of 50 meters—will help develop speed.

Most experts believe that limiting the actual number of vaults, particularly during the competitive season, is key to reducing "burn out" or the risk of injury.

GLOSSARY

Fosbury Flop (FAHS BER ee FLAHP) — a revolutionary style of high jumping invented in the 1960s by American Olympic champion Dick Fosbury, which features a lay-out position over the bar, instead of the traditional face-down scissor kick

horizontal velocity (HAWR eh ZAHNT ul vuh LAHS ut ee) — a scientific way of saying "running speed"

J-hook (JAY HOOK) — the curving approach of a high jumper to the bar, different from the straightaway approach used by all other jumpers

meter (MEET er) — units of measure in the "metric" system used in international competition to measure distances in races and throws and jumps; a meter is just over one yard (39.37 inches versus 36 inches)

plant box (PLANT BAHKS) — the standard launch apparatus at the end of the runway where a pole vaulter sticks ("plants") the point of the vaulting pole before leaving the ground

GLOSSARY

rock back (RAHK BAK) — technique used by a pole vaulter after the plant, swinging both feet forward into the air, pointing both feet at the bar to begin the ascent to the jump's high point

runway (RUN WAY) — a long strip used in such events as long jump, triple jump, and pole vault, which athletes use as an approach lane

scoring zone (SKAWR ing ZON) — the landing pit for long and triple jumpers, made of sand

takeoff board (TAYK AWF BAWRD) — a board across the runway, measuring eight inches (about 20 centimeters) by four feet (about 1.25 meters) beyond which the jumper (long and triple) may not step on takeoff

vertical lift (VERT eh kul LIFT) — a scientific way of saying "lift" or "jumping ability"

FURTHER READING

Find out more with these helpful books and information sites:

Bowerman, William J. and Freeman, William H. *High Performance Training for Track and Field,* Human Kinetics, 1990

Carr, Gerry A. *Fundamentals of Track and Field,* Human Kinetics, 1991

Dick, Frank W. et al. *High Jump,* Tafnews Press, 1993

Jacoby, Ed and Fraley, Bob. *Complete Book of Jumps,* Human Kinetics, 1995

Koch, Edward R. *USA Track and Field Directory,* USATF, 1993

Tricard, Louise Mead. *American Women's Track and Field: A History 1895-1980,* McFarland & Company, 1996

American Track and Field Online at
    www.runningnetwork.com/aft/

M-F Athletic Company at
    www.mfathletic.com (an online catalog for track and field books,
    tapes, clothes, etc.)

Track and Field News at
    www.trackandfieldnews.com/

United States of America Track and Field at
    www.usatf.org

INDEX